FOR SUCCESSFUL SOCIAL MEDIA

100 Lessons

to

Grow Your Business

Using Social Media

Tracey Warren

Ready, Set, Grow Marketing

Readysetgrowmarketing.com

Debbie -
Stay Social
Tracey Warren

Six-Word Lessons for Successful Social Media – 6wordlessons.com
Editing by Patty Pacelli

Copyright © 2013 by Tracey Warren

Published by Pacelli Publishing
9905 Lake Washington Blvd. NE, #D-103
Bellevue, Washington 98004
Pacellipublishing.com

ISBN-10: 1-933750-32-4
ISBN-13: 978-1-933750-32-3

Twitter. Facebook. Linkedin. Google. Four phrases that in the 20th century meant nothing to entrepreneurs looking to market their businesses. Now in the 21st century, phrases like these comprise the hub of marketing strategies from mom and pop shops to the largest of multinational corporations. Enter the era of Social Media.

The Social Media choices available to entrepreneurs today are daunting to say the least. Executed well, entrepreneurs are able to drive much greater cost-effective business results than they ever could have achieved using traditional marketing methods. Executed poorly, entrepreneurs waste precious time and money chasing fads that don't reach their targets. This is why I wrote **Six-Word Lessons for Successful Social Media**.

Six-Word Lessons for Successful Social Media contains 100 handy, easy-to-understand tips that can help anyone looking to learn how to use Social Media in their marketing campaigns do so quickly and effectively. Each lesson is simple, concise, and to-the-point, written by someone who has lived and breathed Social Media since its inception. Rather than pore through pages and pages of theory and questionable advice, **Six-Word Lessons for Successful Social Media** will help you get the nuggets you need to put you on the road to designing and implementing a cost-effective Social Media strategy that delivers results.

I hope you are able to learn from and use some of the ideas in this book, and I wish you success in your Social Media endeavors. Let me know how it has impacted you at tracey@readysetgrowmarketing.com.

Six-Word Lessons for Successful Social Media

Table of Contents

Social Media is Here to Stay

1

Why this book?
Why right now?

Are you feeling confused, frustrated or downright overwhelmed at the prospect of starting and maintaining an active, engaging, valuable and PROFITABLE Social Media presence?

Maybe what you need is something simple to help you get started down the right path.

Look no further.

2

Why should I bother or care?

The numbers are huge, unfathomable really, and just getting bigger. But, it isn't about the numbers. It's about finding clients and customers for your product or service. In almost every instance, and for almost every business, you can find those people using Social Media.

3

Answering the elusive question of ROI

When we started using phones for business, no one asked about the Return on Investment (ROI), but we also know that you need to have a phone for business. A telephone is a tool, just like Social Media. The ROI is in the long term relationships being built through this tool.

4

Social Media is all about opportunity.

It's not an absolute. When you send an e-mail, you can be fairly certain it is received. Social Media is a bit different. It's about opportunity and about creating brand recognition and the online reputation we all need.

5

Be willing to join the conversation.

The conversations are happening right now...maybe without you. Be willing to jump in, join the conversation, heck--START the conversation! The community that you create using Social Media can differentiate you, not only in your neighborhood, but also in your industry.

6

Social Media levels the playing field.

Because using Social Media is financially free, it gives everyone the opportunity to play. Whether your "competition" is just around the corner, or across the ocean, Social Media allows you to be equals, with access to the same tools and platforms.

7

Not to impress, but impress upon.

Bragging is unbecoming--and nowhere is that more obvious than on social channels. If you want to be successful, save your brags for your mastermind groups! When businesses spend most of their time talking about their newest clients, it acts as a repellant to prospects.

8

Sales and marketing aren't the same.

When Social Media first appeared, many sales people thought, "This is great, another place to broadcast my promotions!" Not exactly. Marketing is about messaging and in this case, relationship building. Sales is about what you do with the prospect after they have heard your message.

9

Start with strategy, build with tactics.

The first question you should ask yourself before you start marketing on Social Media is "Why?" What are you hoping to accomplish? Who are you trying to reach? Hint: The answer shouldn't be, "to grow my business." What more can you offer by being social?

10

Keep your eyes on the opportunity.

Opportunities abound when you use Social Media to market. You can build relationships, brand recognition, your online reputation, and so much more. The opportunity lies in creating a community that revolves around your business and how that community can support your endeavors.

Pick the Proper Platforms for You

11

Where are your customers and prospects?

There is only so much time in a day, and getting involved on every platform you can find isn't realistic or warranted. You need to know where your current customers and prospects are before you begin. The next handful of chapters will serve as a guide to help you decide.

12

Mix online and offline marketing communications.

Social Media is not the end-all for marketing purposes. It is just one piece of the pie. And, those businesses that mix online and offline presence and communications will see the most success. Don't forget to make it social!

13

Facebook, friends and a Business Page

On Facebook, it's imperative that you create a Business Page for your business. Having a "friend" page for your business not only limits the information you have for each person from a demographics perspective, but it also violates Facebook Terms, which means your page could be deleted without notice.

14

You can't argue with one billion.

Actually, you can, but you would probably lose. Facebook has over one billion users and over half of them log in every day. Chances are, your best customer, advocate or referral partner is spending part of his day there.

15

Twitter is not just a microblog.

Many businesses use Twitter as a "broadcast platform." And, with its 140 character limit, you may not see it as a place for more than that. But, those who are doing it right see Twitter as just another way to communicate and build relationships.

16

For live, active results, search Twitter.

If you want to know what people are talking about in regard to your service or product, start with a Twitter search. You can discover what people are talking about right now, and join in the conversations. On Twitter, it's perfectly O.K. to interrupt.

17

Use video to tell your story.

The home base for video sharing is YouTube. And, because they are owned by Google, they are a force. All businesses need to be found, and sharing video on YouTube is a great way to facilitate that. If you are sharing a business message, make sure it's short enough that people won't mind taking the time out to watch.

18

Look beyond YouTube for sharing video.

While YouTube is the standard for video marketing, the flaw is that when people see your video, they also can see the competition. Be sure to check out sites like Vimeo, UStream, Viddler and others for your video needs. They aren't as popular, but they offer options not available on YouTube.

19

Pinterest drives traffic to your website.

Pinterest isn't just the next greatest Social Media phenomenon. It is also a traffic creation machine. Product and service-based businesses are seeing amazing web traffic based on their Pinterest activities, such as posting blogs, photos and even videos with links back to their website.

20

Can my company benefit from Pinterest?

If you use photos and videos to sell your product or service, the answer is a resounding YES! Every "pin" can include a link to your home base. (website or blog) And, with the addictive nature of Pinterest, i.e., lots of shiny things, chances are good that your posts will be seen, liked and re-pinned.

21

Make impact with personal search results.

Having a presence on Google Plus is imperative if you have a location and want additional benefits from search results. When you are logged into your Google account, the search results you get are personalized and will include posts from Google Plus.

22

Google Plus offers some great features.

While much less active, Google Plus cannot be ignored. There are some great features like Google Hangouts, where you can video chat with multiple people at one time, and great event promotion that integrates with your Google Calendar and sends e-mail reminders.

23

Don't overlook the power of LinkedIn.

When discussing Social Media, many leave out the business powerhouse that is LinkedIn. If you are looking to connect with specific businesses, people in specific roles within a business, or simply trying to build your expertise, all can be accomplished with a small amount of effort on LinkedIn.

24

Blogging helps create your expert status.

Blogging definitely needs to be a part of the Social Media marketing discussion. Your blog gives you a better opportunity to tell stories, educate your audience and connect with them on a level deeper than the snippet that other platforms allow.

25

Blog titles make all the difference.

A well written blog title can be the difference between your blog being read and spread or sitting in your archives unseen. Use great keywords, make them easier to share and allow readers to comment. Also, better to keep titles short! If people are sharing on Twitter, short is best.

26

Use e-mail marketing as another touch.

Contrary to popular myth, e-mail is still a great tool for communicating with your clients and potential clients. And, most platforms offer integration that will allow people to join your list directly from your Facebook page.

27

There are dozens of other options.

We have talked about the big platforms, where the most people are playing. It would suit you well to also pay attention to Instagram, Tumblr, Reddit and many others like it. Younger users are very active on these platforms. If that is part of your target audience, it would be worth your time to do some research.

Define Your Strategy, Work Your Plan

28

Are you easy to find online?

You should look. Stop right now and Google yourself, search on Bing and Yahoo, too. Does your business show up on the first page? If not, the good news is you can easily move up from where you are. Take note of where you show up, put this book into practice and watch your business move up the ranks in those results!

29

Start with the end in mind.

What are your business goals? Do you have a marketing plan? Where does Social Media fit into that? What do you hope to accomplish? Do you want to solidify current relationships and partnerships or build new ones? Or both?

Knowing where you want to go from the start is the best way to create a strategy and move forward.

30

Create a community around your business.

When you share great content, you build a following, or a community, around your business. You can grow that community through sharing about your business partners and others you trust. When you do that, you get known as a resource--and that is a great thing to be known for.

31

It's a marathon, not a sprint.

You don't plant a seed and then yell at it to sprout and grow. Treat Social Media marketing like a garden and you will be much more realistic and happy with the results. Plant seeds in the activity, cultivate the relationships and you will reap the rewards you are looking for.

32

Use Social to build your expertise.

To become an expert, one usually spends thousands of hours in their field. All of that knowledge and information can be shared on Social Media. That knowledge also allows you to answer questions and address your topic online.

33

Social Media is not about campaigns.

Oftentimes, you hear Social Media marketing companies talk about campaigns, or short bursts of activity to promote a certain event or activity. Those campaigns may have a short term effect, but as I hope to show you, this isn't a limited activity, but rather an integral and integrated part of your marketing for the long haul.

34

Remember the people behind your company.

People want to do business with other people, and Social Media gives you a way to highlight those people in your company-- even if your company is just you! Be sure to include pictures and personalities of those people! It helps customers and potential customers get to know who you are.

35

Create, develop, and sustain great relationships.

One of the first steps to creating and developing great relationships is to show up and be yourself. Be who you are in real life online. If you send mixed messages, it creates suspicion and doesn't breed trust.

36

Measure and refine, change when necessary.

How do you know if your efforts are working? There are a few indicators to pay attention to. Are your Google rankings improving? Are people liking, commenting and sharing on your activity? Are you getting good referrals? If not, it may be time for an evaluation and change.

37

Information is cheap, meaning has value.

The information you need is out there for you and your customers, but there is value in providing meaning to that information. How can you make your information unique so that your potential customer or advocate can use it?

38

Focus on pull, rather than push.

We have a sale! Buy this! Come here! No one likes to be sold to, but everyone loves to buy. But, don't push with sales messages. Give them great information and it will pull them into this community you are creating.

39

Ask them how you can help.

Are you aware of the best ways you can serve your audience? What are they wondering about? What concerns might they have? What is their pain? You have the opportunity to address any or all of these in your activities on Social Media.

40

Ask them if they can help.

Are you launching a new product, a new workshop, have writers block? Wondering if your fans will respond? ASK THEM! People love the opportunity to share their opinion and will happily share theirs if you just ask.

41

Then, ask them to help you.

If you treat your Social Media as a resource for building relationships, over time you will build advocates and cheerleaders for your brand. When you manage it properly and you do need help, those people who already love you and your brand will gladly come to the rescue.

42

Invite people to ask you questions.

Make your Social Media a place where your potential customers and clients can come to get their questions answered. Answering those questions in a timely manner shows that you aren't just good at what you do, a true "expert"--but also that you want to help. It really shows you care.

43

Blog in response to people's questions.

One of the biggest challenges business owners face is how to create new, fresh, relevant content on a regular basis. Social Media makes it easy to solicit questions, gather opinions and get feedback and you can take that information and use it to create blog posts.

44

Done is always better than perfect.

I get it. You are the business owner and you want it to be just right. Don't let the perfect words, the perfect strategy or the perfect promotion get in the way to taking action right now.

45

Set yourself up as the expert.

Trust happens at the speed of Social Media right now. After meeting you, someone can search for you and quickly establish whether or not they want to do business. Your blog, Facebook page, Twitter account, website, etc., help you establish your expertise--sometimes 140 characters at a time.

Build Your Brand, Grow Your Business

46

What story are your profiles telling?

Before we start talking about building your brand, you will want to see what your profiles are already saying about you. What do you want to be known for? Those key words, business roles and primary activities should be similar on each platform where you are active.

47

Please don't obsess about the numbers.

When you first start your Facebook page and Twitter account, it's easy to get obsessed with watching the count. "How many fans do I have today?" "Why don't I have more?" "Why aren't my friends liking my page?" The truth is, not all your friends will like you page or follow you and that is O.K. Many of your friends may not be great prospects, either.

48

Focus on quality instead of quantity.

This isn't a race to get as many likes and followers as possible. I would rather have 1,000 fans that love my brand and are advocates than 10,000 who clicked like just because. In fact, studies have shown that the bigger the numbers, the more challenging it is to get that engagement we need.

49

Make your presence a business asset.

Making it an asset does not mean you have thousands of fans and followers. Those are just numbers. What makes it an asset is the activity, the engagement and the "people talking about us." If those aren't there, you have an inactive web presence that will take work to make it into an asset, but don't worry, it can be done.

50

People do business with other people.

Questions often arise about whether Social Media is good for B2B or B2C, but the truth is, business is about P2P. Ultimately, we want to do business with people, and the more businesses treat their fans and followers like people instead of prospects, the more success they will have.

51

Drive traffic to your great website!

Your website should always be the hub or home base for your business. You can always use Social Media to drive traffic to your website. Point them to different pages, new features, etc. What's great about this tactic is if the analytics on your website are set up correctly, you will be able to see the results from this activity.

52

Being "liked" is just the beginning.

I can't say this anymore plainly that that. Having the "like" isn't like signing a contract, but the person who has willingly engaged with you is now part of your audience. They've opted in and now you have the chance to shine!

53

Respond to positive and negative feedback.

Many businesses avoided Social Media in the beginning because they were worried about what people might say about them. The truth is, if they want to say bad things, they will. It's how you respond that will allow your character to show itself. Always respond humbly with the heart to help.

54

Social keeps you top of mind.

When you post content on a nearly daily basis, it's a virtual tap on someone's shoulder, or drip--but the best kind of drip. You are sharing great information and tips, and when someone needs you they will remember the value you've given.

55

Keep your focus on building relationships.

Yes, I'm talking about using Facebook for your business. If you are using Social Media to "build your list" it will be obvious. If you keep your focus on people and relation-ships, you will see the most success.

Want More Impact? Try These Tactics

56

Be consistent with your business posts.

When a business is active on a daily basis (or nearly every day) they send a message that they are active, available and able to help a customer or potential client quickly. People are coming to expect this sort of customer service.

57

Use Social to thank people personally.

Never has so much information been available about so many people online as right now. With a quick search through Facebook, Twitter and Pinterest, it can be fairly easy to figure out favorite music, coffee, flower, birthday, etc. from your favorite clients and prospects. Thank them personally and you will be unforgettable.

58

Use language appropriate for each platform.

Symbols like # and @ are perfectly appropriate for Twitter, but ONLY for Twitter. LinkedIn and Facebook users prefer everyday language. (Although this may be subject to change as these platforms evolve.)

59

For best effectiveness, stop clicking like.

It takes less than a second to click "like" and yours may or may not be seen. If you comment, it doesn't take a lot of time, but ALWAYS gets noticed. Even if your comment is a one-word response, it shows you took the time to say something.

60

Use these four words for impact.

"This week we helped." These are some of the most powerful words you can use on Social Media. They help tell your story in a non-threatening way that causes people to consider those in their life who might need to be helped in the same way.

61

Turn online friendships into offline relationships.

The more connected we become digitally, the more we crave that personal touch. Pick up the phone, schedule a lunch or coffee date, go to networking events. You might be surprised at the impact the offline activities can produce for your business. Don't be too busy to be social in real life.

62

Know your keywords and use them.

It's easy on Social Media to see the interactions. What you don't see is that when you use your keywords and are active online, you are rewarded by search engines with higher rankings. We will talk more about search in an upcoming chapter.

63

Who is talking about your business?

You can know for sure by using tools like Google Alerts. (google.com/alerts) GA can be set up to notify you when your name or business appears in online publications. This works especially well if you have a more unique name. If your name is John Smith, you are out of luck.

64

Play where your prospects are playing.

It can be tempting to feel like you need to be represented on every Social Media site, and maybe over time, you can invest in using a number of sites, but start small. Figure out where your prospects and their connections are hanging out and start there. Having a profile on LinkedIn and a business page on Facebook are good starting points.

65

The key is to have conversation.

Ask questions, get feedback, get opinions. In this digital marketplace, it's easy to feel like your thoughts, feelings and opinions don't matter much. There is great opportunity for businesses that value those connections as relationships instead of prospects.

66

Third party posting apps hurt engagement.

Many advocate for using third party posting tools to type your message in once and have it broadcast to every platform you use, but these tools hurt engagement. On Facebook, these posting tools can be blocked as well.

67

Be aware of your personal limitations.

If you want a Social Media presence, but cannot see time in your business day to make it happen, that's O.K. You may want to look into hiring a virtual assistant who can help manage your online presence.

Create a Community, Connect, Engage, Care

68

You will win when you listen.

A staggering 90 percent of business posts are not responded to. If you can take two to five minutes a day to check and see if someone has written to you, (checking Facebook, Twitter, LinkedIn and Google Plus) and respond to their activity, you will be well on your way to building great rapport and community.

69

Use photos to draw people in.

Photos can be pleasing to the eye and also a break from the rows and rows of plain text that can plague Facebook. Use them properly and they can accentuate your posts and help convey the message.

70

Post and respond like someone's watching.

At times, Social Media can seem a bit lonely. It can be a long, slow process. Even worse, it can feel like no one is even paying attention. But, know they are!

71

Create brand ambassadors, advocates and evangelists.

An amazing thing happens when you use Social Media effectively, you build a following--but not just any following. These raving fans know you and your business, can offer help and defense when needed, and are often the first to share your content with their networks.

72

Get seen, shared and sought after.

Visibility has never been more important than it is now. Social Media makes us more visible, and that visibility, in a community with advocates and supporters, can mean greater opportunity for you and your business.

73

Don't take your fans for granted.

When your fans respond to your posts, share your content and otherwise engage, be sure to say thank you. Saying thanks is the surest way to encourage the behavior to continue.

Find the Tools that Work for You

74

Improve your search rankings with posts.

Did you know that your activity on Social Media is all cataloged by the major search engines? Most businesses have websites that don't change very often, but Social Media does and your business activity can be rewarded in your search rankings!

75

How are people searching for you?

Ask your clients, "What words would you use to search for my business?" The words they use might surprise you, but can also offer valuable feedback as you plan and market your business. The Google Adwords tool is one way to see what words people are using and can be helpful in addition to other feedback.

76

Know the best times to post.

Go to a search engine right now and search for, "When are the best times to post on Facebook?" and you will get dozens of opinions, which may or may not be relevant to your business. Instead, post at different times of the day to see how YOUR audience responds. Then, post accordingly.

77

Know the best content to post.

This will take a little more testing to understand. Post a variety of content, pictures, quotes, articles, etc. What does your audience respond to? What causes them to react and respond? Take note and post more of that type of content.

78

Use posting tools best for listening.

HootSuite and Tweetdeck are two of the bigger names in posting tools and I'm an advocate of using them to post on Twitter, but they are more helpful as listening tools. Want to make sure you always see information from specific people? Choose one of these tools to help.

79

Use video to tell your stories.

When it comes to social and search, there is no argument that video is one of the most powerful tools. Remember, Google owns YouTube. Share your stories in one to five minute segments.

80

Videos should look compelling to play.

Have a great title for your video, one that truly represents what they will see. In addition, the video should be made with good quality sound and lighting. This is the online representation of you. Make it count, but don't get caught up in making it perfect, either. Authenticity is more important than perfection.

Get it Done in Less Time

81

Facebook isn't really a time-suck.

You own your time, so establish some limits and a plan that allow you to use the tools, but not get sucked in for hours on end. Block games, people who aren't serving you, and activities you don't wish to see.

82

Set a timer
if you must.

Give yourself fifteen to thirty minutes a day. Check in on the platforms you've chosen. Post an article, a status, a note. Touch base with current clients and prospects--then move on!

83

Create an editorial social posting calendar.

As a business owner, your cup is likely always running over. A posting calendar can help you drain one item from the cup. Get a blank calendar for each month, and fill it with ideas. What is on your business calendar? Are there are events you are attending? If you plan ahead like this, it will make it simpler to post.

84

Use theme days to simplify posting.

Many businesses do this successfully. Maybe Monday is always a video, Tuesday is a tip, etc. Be creative. Use theme days in partnership with the editorial calendar and that can set you up for time saving and ease.

85

Schedule time for posting and engaging.

When is your most creative time during the day or week? Set some of that time aside for brainstorming subjects you would like to talk about. What challenges seem to keep coming up for clients? Choose a monthly or weekly theme if it helps.

86

To save time, schedule posts ahead.

To post ahead on Twitter or LinkedIn, you can use tools previously mentioned. On Facebook, you can schedule ahead directly on your page. Take advantage of this! If you can schedule time every week or month to schedule ahead, do!

87

Use Twitter Search to find stories.

Let Social Media do some of the work for you. Chances are, people are talking about your topic right now and you can use Twitter search to find great articles and other content, even without a Twitter account. Go to *search.twitter.com* and start curating content!

88

Follow similar businesses with like community.

I'm not advocating stealing directly, but following businesses that are similar to yours or who regularly share content that might also benefit your fans and followers can make your job much easier. Sharing other businesses' content helps build community as well.

89

Block people who fill your feed.

Some of your friends probably like to talk, some of them more than they should. You do have control over what you see in your news feed and one of the settings you can change is what you see from whom. If you have connections who talk too much, you can change the number of posts that will show up. Change to "only important" and that can lighten your feed dramatically.

When in Doubt, Use Common Sense

90

Have a plan for Negative Nellies.

Try as you might, there will always be the complainers. Put a plan into place to deal with them and be consistent. But make sure the plan doesn't include deleting their remarks. That always backfires for businesses. We have seen some great examples of this recently. Never delete negative posts.

91

Respond swiftly to negative feedback.

When the time does come that someone posts a negative comment about you or your business, respond as quickly as possible. Even something as simple as, "We would love to resolve this, can you give us a call." That will speak volumes about who you are and your willingness to work out any challenge.

92

Respond to all feedback with heart.

Business isn't always about heart, but when someone complains, it's the best time to show yours. If you respond with caring and heart, your fans and followers will see it and get to know you even better. But, the truth is, when you truly create a community around your business, those fans will stand up for you!

93

Customers will watch before they hire.

You go to a networking event and you meet someone. They may need to hire you now, but chances are they may not. But, they will find your Social Media channels, and they will watch your work. Are you who you say you are? Do you already have advocates for your brand? When you stay top of mind, those potentials customers will call you when they have a need.

94

Think of Social Media as social business.

Social Media is just an extension of you and your brand. It is a part of the marketing plan; and when done correctly can leverage your business in amazing ways. So, it isn't just Social Media—it's how your business is represented in an online forum.

95

Don't violate the Terms of Service.

Be sure to at least scan the Terms of Service (especially on Facebook, as it has the most rules). Violating any of these rules can have your page deleted with no recourse. Pay special attention to information about contests!

96

Don't tell fans you're on vacation.

Tell your fans you are on vacation, and they will take one as well--from interacting with you and your page. If you've created an editorial posting calendar, (see lesson number 86) you can post ahead, so your fans won't even know you are gone. You can stay top-of-mind, even if you are not online.

97

Be careful about contests on Facebook!

There are very specific rules for how to hold a contest on Facebook, and violating those rules can get your page shut down permanently. Always use a third party contest application and that will keep you safe.

98

Fans and followers aren't just prospects.

O.K., the truth is, maybe for some of you they are. But, never EVER treat them that way. They will see right through your schemes and run the other way.

99

Don't be part of the noise.

There are thousands of businesses adding to the noise online with their "Buy this," or, "Call me about this." With the tips, tricks and tools in this book, you can be above the noise, and by doing so, can make HUGE impact.

Social Media Takes Time, Don't Quit

100

It's not about get rich quick.

This is a long process. Try some of the recommendations here, then watch, but don't give up. Lather, rinse, repeat and be willing to change based on reactions. And don't be afraid to reach out for help if you decide you need it.

See the entire Six-Word Lesson Series at
6wordlessons.com

Want to learn more about Social Media?

Contact Tracey at
readysetgrowmarketing.com

Read more about Tracey at
readysetgrowmarketing.com

Made in the USA
Charleston, SC
15 April 2013